BEYOND HERE THERE BE MIRACLES

Part 2

Richard Mulligan

ISBN-13: 978-0-473-73541-8

CONTENTS

OVERIEW OF PREVIOUS EVENTS

Please ignore this if you have already read "Beyond Here There Be Miracles Part 1."

Please ignore this if you have already read "Beyond Here There Be Miracles Part 1."

In Part 1, I outlined why and how I became a Christian after chasing after my own ambitions and pleasure for at least ten years. If you know me, when I commit to something I go full out. This meant I went to Missionary training college within two years of becoming a Christian again and subsequently ended up in Paris, France, as a missionary.

I spent two and a half years there working with a local Elim church, specifically looking after their 'University age' people. God did amazing things with those people, and in my life, with many instances of miraculous provision. It was in Paris that I met my future wife, Louisa, who hailed from Denmark.

After Louisa and I were married we lived in Denmark for almost a year and a half. God was continuing to guide and we saw incredible answers to prayer. We were attending the Copenhagen Vineyard - Louisa had been going there since she'd come back from Paris the year before and she was loving it! It was fantastic, God had Louisa happily and firmly involved in the Vineyard, long before I arrived in Denmark.

Louisa came from a conservative Lutheran back ground, so I was a little concerned about how she would react to my much more

Charismatic approach, especially with regard to the Holy Spirit. God took care of all that, the first time she went to the Vineyard the Holy Spirit came on her, and she cried and cried. She didn't even know why, the Holy Spirit was doing a healing work deep in her, she felt and knew the love and peace of God.

The people there were amazing and with under 100 people it was an intimate gathering and people knew each other. After I arrived, Louisa and I held a home group at our apartment where we had Bible Studies, lively discussions, and prayed for each other. A mind blowing fact at this time, (which we didn't realise till later) was that EVERY prayer request we made in that group was answered! Big ones, small ones, God came through, though sometimes it took time. After about six to nine months Louisa and I began to suspect there was something special going on. It wasn't until about fifteen months after we started that we were talking about it one night at home group and we realised God had answered EVERY prayer we'd agreed on as a group.... Wow! Talk about faith building.
One of the bigger ones, especially for Louisa and I, was to get an apartment in Copenhagen. It was incredibly difficult, we had been putting out feelers for almost six months to try and get a rental or a cheaper half rent / half ownership place (almost impossible) to absolutely no avail! The day we had to move out was coming closer and closer and we were having no luck.

We were praying about it, but nothing materialised, so we were thinking maybe God wanted us to live with Louisa's parents for a while. Though that seemed a bit desperate and made no sense. With 2 weeks till we HAD to be out of the place we were renting, we thought why not look at buying a place (even though we had no money and no deposit). So in a kind of crazy desperation we started to look at places that we could maybe, with a miracle, afford. Even looking at buying - there was very little available, especially in our price bracket.

Looking through the real estate paper we identified three

possibles in different parts of Copenhagen, two in Armager, where we were currently renting a place. With just over a week to go, the first miracle occurred, we heard from NZ that enough money to cover the minimum deposit would be made available to us. Praise God!

We booked in viewings on the Monday night for both places in Armager. We'd already looked and discounted one that was out the other side of Copenhagen. The apartment had been nice but was located right on a very busy, noisy, main road and it was outside of Copenhagen itself, in not a great area.

On the Monday night of the week we HAD to move out Friday, we got on our trusty bikes to check out the two options. We had continued to ask people and apply for rentals, and the cheaper half rent/ownership options, but there was nothing. At this stage we were pretty much resigning ourselves to living in Hillerod with Louisa's parents, it seemed impossible. But God. We had never heard of anyone, in Denmark, getting a place to move into within a week, never mind the three days we had!

The first place for sale was in a desirable central Armager location but it was tiny, quite old and wouldn't be available, even if we could come to an agreement, for at least three months. The owner laughed and said that moving in within six weeks would be impossible, not only with her but with any place we looked at. Even so, it was top of our possibles list as we could probably cope going in and out from Hillerod each day for a couple of months, if we knew it was for a set time period.

Next we tried what we thought was a long shot, it was a private sale, by a young Arab guy, so we weren't sure what to expect. A 'private sale' meant all the Danish alarm bells were ringing! Anyway the 'bare details' we had seen in the paper seemed reasonable, so away we headed to Lyneborgade 4, 4 TV.

We went up and the young guy greeted us, he was quite friendly, especially when he realised I was a foreigner too. We looked at the place, which was empty. Ok, the shower was literally a tiny converted closet in the bedroom, but the rest was great and being on the highest level was a bonus. Louise and I had a brief conversation and I approached the guy and said, well we really like it - I know it's a private sale - what now?

He said "When do you want to buy and move in?"

I said, "Ahhh I know this is a bit crazy, but this Friday?"

"Oh, well, as you can see, I've already moved out and there's no sense in it being empty while the lawyers take their time over the agreement, (minimum six weeks).
Why don't you rent it off me for the first 2-3 months and then we can take the rental off the final price?"

I'm stunned, "Really?! Sure, that sounds fantastic!"

So we shook hands and he gave us the keys, right there and then! We just needed to put the 2 months rent in his account by that Friday and we could move straight in.

WHAT??!!!!
Everyone was both horrified and amazed! They had NEVER heard of anything like this happening, ever, and being able to move in that same week was a miracle. Some of our family were super suspicious - they thought he was trying to rip us off somehow. In Denmark you DO NOT do anything without the official sign off, abundant paperwork and authorisation. To all of them it was crazy-bonkers, buying an apartment with a handshake and moving in the same week! It was only because both he and I were foreigners that it worked, a Dane never, never, would have either sold, or bought the apartment on a handshake. Thank you Lord! God bless that young guy!

Our lawyers couldn't believe it either, and even advised us we should pull out of the agreement and do a new 'official' one, just in case something didn't work out. Luckily I was a foreigner too, so both of us could do the unthinkable and honour our word and handshake. Later on, they said that his lawyers had made a 'mistake' and that we could capitalise on it and claim more 'expenses' off the initial price, but we said we were sticking to the initial deal as that was the right thing to do. It turned out it was fortunate we didn't wait the time till all was legal and official to move in, as it took ten weeks to finalise.

That apartment was such a blessing to us, we had the home group there and lots of people around. It was in a great location and was pretty close to everything in Copenhagen.

The finances were another miracle, first one of my Paris missionary supporters gave us, yes gave us, the initial deposit (approx $NZ 25,000). Then I'd had a full time job for two months so it looked like we were making enough income to pay the mortgage, the job only lasted three and a half months, but was enough to get us a mortgage.

After about six months in the apartment, things started to get a bit tight, I was down to minimum hours for my new job teaching Business English and Louisa was finishing her Masters. We were praying about it and one day I got a call from a friend of mine in New Zealand who said I should work for a Christian friend of his in New Zealand, this friend was working crazy hours and needed someone to work alongside him and help. The best part was it was based in Cambridge, where my parents lived. Long story short, Craig was keen for me to work for him and after being sent to the parent company in Germany for an interview they were keen too. So in the European summer of 2001 we headed back to live in Cambridge NZ.

Please bear in mind:

"This could be anyone's story. I'm just an ordinary person, with weaknesses, who's happy to have a relationship with an extraordinary God. This could be you…"

PARIS AGAIN?

We'd been back in NZ for almost 5 years living in the town I'd grown up in, Cambridge. We were there mainly because of my parents; my father had suffered two major head injuries in the late 1980's and was still a damaged and broken shadow of the man he once was. Living in Cambridge meant that Louise could get to know my parents and my sister, (who lived in a nearby city) and I was around to give my mother support with Dad when she needed it.

In Christmas 2005 Louise's parents decided to come out to NZ to see us. Our daughters were two and a half and fifteen months old and were super cute. We had a great Christmas and they loved spending quality time with their granddaughters, so when they left it was understandable and inevitable that Louise missed her family and felt homesick for Denmark. It's tough when all your immediate family is overseas, you don't have the same support systems. My parents were fine, but being older and with Dad's injury they couldn't really cope taking care of boisterous toddlers.

In February 2006 we were sitting in our 'home office' (I had been in Real Estate for a year at the time) and I said if you're missing your family that much why don't we go back to Denmark for a holiday. We impulsively looked up the cost of flights and it came back at around NZ$12,000! I said, "That's crazy! – for that price we could just move there!" Louise's eyes caught mine and we both had the same thought – actually, maybe we should move back. On the surface, the idea seemed a bit out there, but we agreed that we should at least consider the option and pray about it. Maybe now was the right time to go back to Europe and follow up the "Paris Vision".

When we were first married and living in Copenhagen, Denmark, we were active participants in the Copenhagen Vineyard. At that time, we'd even discussed with the leadership about going to Paris as part of a Vineyard team, ideally as a church plant of Copenhagen Vineyard.

If returning to Europe was in God, our first port of call was to contact the pastor in Copenhagen. We'd see how things were going and if they'd had any further thoughts about supporting a church plant in another European city. To our profound surprise – he responded from Denmark within hours and said – you won't believe this – he had been talking that same day with Hans (the leader of Vineyard Scandinavia) about Copenhagen supporting a church plant. They'd discussed different options and he had specifically mentioned us and our vision for Paris!

Wow, ok, we've been thinking about returning to Europe, is this the right time? What should we do now? He said to pray and he'd get the ball rolling from his end to see if Vineyard Copenhagen and Scandinavia were keen on the plan. The more we prayed and talked about it – the more certain we were that this was the direction God wanted us to pursue. Though it would be a major change for us, there were a lot of events and circumstances which pointed in that direction. For example, the year before, we'd sold the small house we'd bought not long after we'd arrived in 2001 and our multiple attempts to buy another house had all gone awry. The money we'd made from the house sale, meant we had enough finance to go there – get set up and not need any income for six to nine months. We could get an apartment and get acclimated before I needed to go out and get paid work or enough 'missionary' support.

The pastor contacted the various leaders in Vineyard Europe to gauge their reaction and gain their thoughts. We discovered that the 'rules' on church planting in the Vineyard were just changing and now any Vineyard could plant a church anywhere in Europe. The leaders over an "area" needed to be in agreement with the plan, believe the venture was right, and have people willing to do it. Previously, if we'd wanted to be part of a plant in France we would've gone to England for a year or two, before being sent out to Paris. So being able to be supported and go out as a 'daughter' church of Copenhagen was a huge open door for us.

Over the course of 2006, Vineyard Europe became fully supportive of the plan and the pastor, along with the Vineyard in Copenhagen and Scandinavia, were totally behind us to proceed. Initially, we were thinking of just going to Paris and starting off by setting up a Vineyard house group and taking it from there. However, some of the more experienced leaders suggested that we could be part of a Vineyard evangelisation push called "Paris Je t'aime" (Paris I love you) which was planned for summer 2007.

The major concern for the Vineyard leaders was to have a French couple lead the evangelisation, and start the house group alongside us. This was perfect for us too, as we didn't have church planting experience and we believed local leadership was the best option for a Paris Vineyard's success anyway! Whoop-whoop – we'd head there and set up a 'base' and hopefully get a house group started. Then hopefully, prayerfully, with the evangelisation and the impetus of the French leadership there'd be enough momentum to start a church plant. Exciting!

We were fully aware it was a major challenge; we had 2 young children and as yet no tangible support in Paris – but it looked like God was opening up all the doors. We felt to take steps in faith and trust God to open the way. We remembered God's miraculous provision when I had been in Paris the first time. We continued to pray a lot about it and in faith we booked our tickets for March 22nd 2007.

This gave us plenty of time to prepare, sell up our stuff and send the rest to France. Late in 2006 a twist was added to the adventure, Louise was pregnant again – with our third child, which we found out was going to be a boy.

Time moved on – we were going through all the upheaval of shifting to the other side of the world. We sold almost everything and sent nine cubic metres of the basics to Le Havre, France. It was stressful, especially with a pregnant wife and two small girls!

The people we prayed with and trusted seemed to be encouraging us forward, and we personally had no feelings of uneasiness or checks about moving to Europe. To us it felt like there was continued confirmation to go to France, with little snippets of God showing up. For example, it was uncanny how much of our furniture (including the most comfortable lounge suite in the world) got sold to Christians, most ex-missionaries. In addition, all the logistics of moving to the other side of the world slotted easily into place.

Everything was a 'go' with Copenhagen Vineyard, we'd been discussing and praying about it with the Vineyard Scandinavian leadership. We didn't discuss plans in-depth, but they would support us a bit financially and mentor us through the process. The Copenhagen Vineyard pastor had even mentioned that some younger people from Copenhagen were seriously considering going down to Paris with us, for at least the summer, maybe longer.

We decided that the best thing to do would be to first go to Denmark, reconnect with Louisa's family and the Copenhagen Vineyard people. We were planning to be there for four weeks and during that time I'd head down to Paris for a week and go apartment hunting.

It was sad to be leaving New Zealand after six years – we'd made some fantastic friends and of course my family were there. Fortunately, my family supported us in our 'vision' and so the sadness was tempered by the purpose behind our moving to Europe. It helped that in 2007 there was Skype and a more 'sophisticated' internet to keep in touch.

We arrived in Denmark at the end of March and stayed with Louise's parents who were generally supportive of our plans. They were thrilled to have their daughter and grandkids back in Europe. It felt good to be back and for Louisa to reconnect with her family and for the girls to get to know their relatives. Arianna (three and a half) who in New Zealand was a little confused with the two languages – rapidly became fluent in Danish.

A week later, In April, I headed down to Paris for a week to hunt for an apartment. I would be staying with Jono and his wife, who work for

YWAM. Jono was a kiwi from Hamilton originally and we'd met at his home church, Gateway in Hamilton. We'd stayed in contact, especially after he moved to France and then Paris, to take up the position with YWAM.

A SIGN?

I arrived there during the day and as I came off the metro at their stop (Colonel Fabien) – I realised to my surprise that it was exactly the same stop I'd got off at, nine years previously, when I first went to Paris.

Stepping out of the metro into the hustle and bustle of the Paris streets, it hit me how much I loved being back in Paris again. Being in Paris for me was like coming home – it felt so right to be there. I don't understand it, but I LOVE Paris! It's like I come alive, I feel on fire, like I'm a different person, accessing all of me, fully engaged. The weather was warm (unlike Denmark) and I was revelling in the familiar Parisienne Frenchness of it all as I wandered around trying to find Jono's place.

I finally had to go into a cafe and ring him – as the address seemed to be wrong so he came and got me. We then headed down a street that looked awfully familiar, I asked Jono

"So is this the street you live on?"

"Yeah…" he said.

"Wow.. that's amazing as I'm certain it's the same street I stayed on when I first arrived here nine years ago."

We kept going till we came to his apartment block entrance and with growing incredulity I said " Jono – do you live, here?"

"ahh yeah" he said looking at me like duh … of course I live here, we wouldn't go in here otherwise, Einstein….

"Oh Wow! you're not got to believe this! This is incredible – this is exactly the same apartment complex that I stayed in when I first arrived in Paris!"

"You serious" he said obviously not really getting it.

I on the other hand was getting that prickly feeling on the back of my neck and my smile was a mile wide. We headed up to their apartment and even though I had an inkling, I was still stunned – it WAS the same exact apartment I'd first stayed in nine years ago! What was even more incredible is that the colour scheme and layout was a mirror image of how it had been when I'd stayed there! I gawped around, amazed and speechless.

They were wondering why I was acting so strangely, then as I explained it all to them, the penny dropped and they were as amazed as I was!

They didn't know Andrew from a hill of beans or anything about him and they had only been in the apartment for about nine months themselves. Wow! What are the odds? There are literally millions of places in and around Paris. Another tree was falling and another lion getting squashed. I could almost hear God laughing - welcome back Richard!

It was great to catch up with Jono and talk about NZ and about what God was doing with them and YWAM. Gotta say though guys – I know you love them – but I just don't go warm and gooey over ferrets in the apartment! One of them, little "Missy May" seemed to take a perverse pleasure in biting the new guy's toes – come on they were just sticking out there – all pink and tempting - what's a ferret to do? Ferrets have razor sharp teeth, so it wasn't a friendly little nibble, blood and pain were involved, unfortunately all mine. (Dang, those things are fast).

Great though it was to be with Jono & his French wife Claire; my main reason for being there was to contact as many places as possible to rent an apartment. I was pretty pumped to be back in Paris, especially after the 'apartment coincidence', but I completely struck out on the apartment front – zip, nix, nada. NOTHING, every apartment I looked at was overwhelmed with applicants (twenty to fifty). In addition, I didn't have the two years of French tenant references and salary receipts necessary before they even talked with you. I had plenty of testimonials and references and a healthy bank account, but to no avail. In desperation, I followed up on my previous landlady, only to find out she'd died a few years previously. Huh?! That was a shock, we'd got on well, she hadn't retired and seemed in pretty good health. What was happening here? I even went around to my old apartment building, but things had changed and there was no 'concierge' anymore to ask anything.

After running all over Paris for the week, with nothing to show for it, except for a bag of disappointment, I returned to Denmark wondering what the next step should be. Louise and I talked and prayed about it and asked our families and supporters to do the same – The outcome of the different prayers was that we felt encouraged to take a big step of faith, commit to Paris, take the whole family, all our stuff, and go down there. Gulp…

With the decision made, I looked on the net and in a couple of hours we'd landed a great apartment in a good location for a short-term rental of 4 weeks. She was Swedish and he French and they were really happy that we would be looking after their place while they were off on holiday. Major bonus, they even had a real 'espresso' machine! (side note: if you haven't had espresso coffee for a few weeks, do not go all out the first day like I did… lets say there are consequences).

Perfect - it seemed like the doors were opening again. An extra bonus was that Louise's sister and brother in law decided to come down with us for the first few days to help out, as they'd never been to Paris before. So only a week after my return back from Paris, we all flew down – yikes!

Emilie & Morten you were a God-send. We'd brought a tonne of luggage from New Zealand as we were intending to live in Paris. In hindsight, it was far too much for us to handle with two young girls and a wife who was seven months pregnant! The extra hands were not only welcome, but necessary, it would have been impossible without them.

After we landed, we had to wait a long time for the train into the city and then the metro was hot and crowded. It was too much for Isabella

– she was so tired and upset that she threw up – poor girl. Paris, and the Metro especially, were pretty scary for the girls, there were almost no kids, lots of strange looking people and unlike NZ, people weren't as open and friendly in public. We were so glad to finally arrive at the place we were to stay, after four hectic transfers from one metro line to another. The couple were surprisingly nice and understanding and they were quickly off on their holiday. There we were, exhausted, in our accommodations, all 50m2 of it. The location was great, though it was in an area neither Louisa nor I were familiar with.

Living in Paris compared to New Zealand (especially Cambridge) took a huge adjustment, particularly for the girls. Paris in general is much dirtier, but the metro was down right nasty. We needed to get into the habit of washing our hands every time we came home, NOT their favourite thing after walking all over Paris in the heat and walking up the four flights of stairs! They were intimidated by all the people, particularly the Africans (totally not used to them in NZ or Denmark). It was freaky for them to see beggars, homeless and alcoholics on the streets, made worse because most were more than a few sandwiches short of a picnic. They'd see some filthy, reeking, dishevelled guy on a bench or slumped beside a wall, shaking his head, talking to himself waving his arms around or shouting randomly at passers by. Definitely a huge shock to their systems.

But the Croissants! Ahhhh.. They almost made up for it, Morten and I made a concerted effort to try out as many bakeries as possible, (Tough assignment). Come on, fresh Paris croissants (definitely plural) with espresso coffee or latte - divine. It ended up that the best place was just down the road from where we were staying - how awful! In our search we found a place in the 15th arrondissement that made a melt in your mouth, absolutely heavenly "Mille Fois'. It was the best Morten and I have ever tasted. Even now many years later I haven't had a better one. (Ok, ok, I admit, years later when I returned to Paris for a visit, I spent a few hours and a few Euro's sampling and looking for the place. I didn't find it, so If anyone knows where it is, please share! I think it was in the 15th, they focused more on cakes and pastries than a normal Paris bakery.)

We were so blessed by Emilie & Morten those days they were with us - we couldn't have coped without them, they were angels. After they left, the following week my cousin Geoff and his wife, Sarah Claire came over from Ireland and they were a God send too! They bought toys and stuff for the kids and Sarah Claire was fantastic with Louisa, giving her support as it was quite difficult being pregnant in a city like Paris in the heat of summer.

Meanwhile, I contacted more rental agencies and followed up where I could, expanding the search all over Paris. We applied for apartments, we even managed to see a few, but all to no avail, there was nothing available for us.

The only sliver of a possibility was outrageously expensive, and they would require us to post a Euro 40,000 bond up front. Rent wasn't to be taken out, but rather paid on top of that every month so there would always be a Euro 40,000 balance, yikes! That was not going to work.

Louisa was also finding it impossible to arrange a hospital to have the baby in. When living in Paris you "book" as soon as you discover you are pregnant, otherwise you can forget it, they'll only take you as an 'emergency' patient at the time of delivery. I couldn't believe how rude and unsympathetic the hospital people were to her. The best they said was that "if she turned up on their doorstep during labour, they'd try and find her a bed, but no guarantees" Pretty heartless.

Exploring all avenues, in the 3rd week there, we met up with a couple from Christchurch who were pastoring a church in the suburbs; they said they could get us a place out in the complex where they were. It was tempting, but we felt strongly that we were meant to stay within the confines of Paris proper, not be 40 mins away in the Northern suburbs. Our rationale was that we were hoping to set up a home group in our own home and we needed to be in Paris itself. I knew of people who had tried living outside of Paris whilst setting up a church inside, and it had failed miserably. I believed it was important to 'find the person of peace' and to reach out to people in the neighbourhood where you live, where your children go to school, so we needed to live in Paris.

At the end of the 3rd week, we decided to visit the recently set up Hillsong church in Paris. Ahh…oops, not quite what we were expecting and not our style (too much in your face and quite "American" even though Hillsong were Australian) but people seemed to enjoy it. One amazing thing happened while we were there. I caught up with an old French friend of mine and got chatting, which led to us being introduced to an angel in human form known as Aubrey; with her husband Peter. Oh my goodness "God bless that woman!" She was phenomenal! She took a discouraged and wilting Louisa and encouraged her, she played with the girls and did everything she could to help us find an apartment. She also introduced us to another American couple that we hit it off with and the wife was a particular encouragement to Louisa in that stressful time.

Fourth week; after trying everything and me running around everywhere, it was down to the last days and still no sign of anything. With one day left in the apartment with heavy hearts (well me anyway) we decided we'd better see if we could get tickets back to Denmark. We couldn't take the plane anymore, as Louisa was too pregnant, so I went to Gare de L'Est to see how soon we could catch a train.

Just before leaving I reminded myself and Louisa of the story (at least this is how i remember it) from Roland Baker, (Iris Ministries). Roland and Heidi had just finished their PHD's and were living in the states but they felt God told them and their team to pack everything up and go to the Philippines. In faith they sold their stuff, moved out of their home, ordered the tickets, packed their suitcases and got everything ready to leave.

The one remaining small issue was that they needed to pay U$10,000 to the travel agent for the tickets. They felt this would be relatively easy, God was clearly leading them, they had a backing church and others, not a problem. But no matter who they asked or whom they talked to, they got stonewalled, the money was not forthcoming. Fortunately, the ticket agent was a Christian and knew they were going out on a mission, so she held off the payment as long as possible, but they were leaving on this coming Saturday, so reluctantly she told them she HAD to know, and have the U$10,000 on the Thursday by 5pm at the latest, otherwise she'd have to sell the tickets to someone else. Roland and Heidi just couldn't figure it out, they'd had lots of financial support over the years, but suddenly when they really needed it, it dried up and even churches which had faithfully supported them were strangely silent. Anyway, with a heavy heart Roland left their friends place where they were staying and walked down to the square to use the payphone, to tell the agent to let the tickets go as they didn't have the money. As he was approaching the phone booth he noticed a limo pull up to the kerb. A tall, handsome man dressed in a tuxedo got out of the car and to his surprise walked over to him. "Roland Baker?" He said,

ahh "Yes" said Roland not knowing who this guy was, or what was happening.

"How big is your faith?" and with that he handed Roland a brown paper bag, turned around and walked over to the Limo and drove off.

Roland, a little confused as to what had just happened, then looked inside the brown paper bag; it was full of cash, U$10,000 of it.

I knew that miracles like that were possible, it had happened to me before in Paris, though not quite on that scale. I knew that at any stage I could get a tap on the shoulder and someone would ask me how big my faith was, and hand me an apartment key.

Now I have to apologise for building you up like that, as I'm sorry to say the tap on the shoulder never came and I bought tickets for the next train to Denmark leaving the following night.

Oops.. slight miss-timing there, we had to move out of the apartment today! What were we to do tonight, with ALL of our luggage. We had a lot more than the normal luggage as we'd brought as much as we could with us in the expectation we would be staying and living in Paris. Yikes! Where were we going to stay tonight? How was I going to get our stuff to the station with two young girls and a heavily pregnant wife...

Enter Aubrey the Angel! (I have said God bless that woman, right?), Aubrey helped to move us out of the temporary apartment and very kindly let us all crash in their small apartment. I had one more shot at an apartment the next day, which didn't work out, but at least it kept me out of everyone's hair for the day. Louisa and Aubrey wrangled the girls and packed us all up (man we had way too much stuff) so we could leave just after lunchtime the next day.

The next day dawned, (with no apartment keys materialising in the night), Peter was off at work, so Aubrey and I loaded ourselves up with at least three or four bags each and staggered off down the street to the Metro Station, which fortunately ran "kind of" directly to Gare de L'Est (there were a couple of connections and a good Kilometre hike from the metro to the international trains) so Aubrey and I were very sweaty and tired by the time we got to the departure platform. Peter joined us there and we bade them a fond farewell, they had been nothing less than angels to us, especially Aubrey. She never once complained and was generous to a fault! (I have said God bless that woman, right?! ☺) well, God Bless her again!

It was a long journey, with a transfer in Germany at 5am! Praise God for another angel in the form of a large black Frenchman named Frank. He must have seen how frazzled and overwhelmed we were with all our stuff. He'd helped us initially on to the train in Paris with our plethora of baggage and boxes, I found it hard to believe that a random stranger could be so kind. I was nearly frantic wondering how we were possibly going to connect with our next train with all our bags, but Frank carried most of our bags to the next train like they weighed nothing, whilst I staggered behind him. Seriously it was a joke, I was doing my best carrying a few bags and nearly falling over and he grabbed all the rest effortlessly like they were airy croissants. Man, I was impressed! God bless that man!

From Germany, it was just five hours later that the train doors opened and waiting for us was Louise's dad Peder Toft. It was such a relief. Familiar territory, Louisa burst into tears and I must admit I felt greatly relieved as well to get back to family in Denmark. We had arrived back safely and Louise was much comforted, especially with the baby literally due in a couple of weeks. She had much needed support from her friends and family as the birth of our third child loomed on the horizon, this was by far an easier option.

A BIENTOT FRANCE, HEJ DANMARK

The first night we were back having dinner with the family, Louisa's sister Kristine said that she might have found me a part-time job! She knew this entrepreneur guy from their church. On top of that, Louisa's parents thought they might know of someone who might sell us a cheap and reliable car (not an easy achievement in Denmark).

Honestly, it was all too easy after France; we did get the car, I did get the job and by the end of that week I had sorted us a likely apartment to rent in Valby, Copenhagen! Huh? We were meant to be living in Paris, then why had all the doors opened so effortlessly when we returned to Denmark? Figure that one.

The next couple of weeks we settled down in Denmark and tried to get our heads around the fact we were going to be living there for the foreseeable future. Foremost in our minds was the imminent birth of our third child.

There was a huge contrast in the attitudes and behaviour between the French and Danish health systems. The local hospital in Hillerod was nothing short of fantastic, Louisa was welcomed with open arms and was assigned an awesome midwife. I have to admit the Danes put even the New Zealand system (which I thought was pretty great) to shame. They scored a perfect 10 in my book.

Note to all aspiring fathers though; if you are going with your wife into theatre for an elective caesarean be warned - it's BRUTAL! It was carnage! I was amazed that they managed to drag (rip more like it, it seemed to me) a whole baby out of there! And I couldn't believe how cavalier they were with Louisa's insides – honestly, I was deeply concerned and kept asking the gay anaesthesiologist if Louisa was ok! "Of course, luv – just relax"

I was more deeply in shock and more scared than when Arianna had been pulled out with forceps. I truly wondered if Louisa was going to make it, she seemed so weak and was totally not with it, besides it looked like she'd exploded! I think because Louisa wasn't coping and was panicking a little, I was freaking out too, it looked horrendous and she seemed so weak. How could anyone recover from such grievous wounds as that. To my immense relief, they did actually know what they were doing, she was ok and a few hours later she and Oliver were both fast asleep in the recovery room. PHEW! I was thanking God I can tell you.

Oliver got his own back though, when the doctor finally got hold of him and dragged him out of his mother, he immediately let rip with a stream of pee over the doctor and nurses!

Oliver was born July 10th 2007 which was the start of the long summer holidays in Denmark, which was great as Louise's parents were teachers and so they had some time off to help us with the girls and moving to Copenhagen.

We got the flat the week after Oliver was born and Louise and baby were back at her parents place recovering. I headed down to Copenhagen to get things set up and to organise some furniture. It wasn't a particularly big place 80 m2 (inc entrance) BUT we had the ultimate of luxuries out the back door – a postage stamp lawn with a sand pit. Your own lawn is BIG news in or near the city in Copenhagen. Ok, let's not mention it was right beside one of the major train stations, with 8 tracks behind us, and one that literally went down the side of the house on a raised bank so the passengers could see down into our kitchen and lawn…. But we had a lawn!

When you get an apartment in Europe things are a little different from New Zealand – they usually take all the fittings. We were fortunate as the owners had left their gas stove, but we had to buy everything else; lights and light fittings, cupboards, shelves, wardrobes, and of course all the normal furniture. Fortunately, a visit to the local IKEA solved most of those issues without cleaning out the bank account. We could rely on the rent to do that, Copenhagen was crazy! In New Zealand (2007), (Cambridge admittedly) we paid $1040 pm for a full house, 3 bedrooms, 2 lounges, 2 bathrooms, with a lawn. In Valby, Copenhagen, NZ$3500 pm for 80m2, 2 bedrooms, on the bottom floor, 1 tiny toilet/ bathroom, in the outer suburbs. Something comparable in NZ, even in downtown Auckland would have been less than half that price. Reality was getting a place in Copenhagen was a big ask at the best of times, so we grabbed the chance with both hands. On the positive side, the train station was just over our shoulder ☺

With much help from Louisa's family, (thank you Mr Toft) we installed ourselves at the end of August and I started biking out to my new part-time job, four hours a day.

Awesome right? Naaah... not so much. I loved the bike ride out there, even though it was forty min each way, as I went through several parks, but the job itself, hmmm...

I worked for an online Danish bookstore, my job was to wrap / pack books that had been ordered. This MUST be done in a precise manner, address label – just so. (no fingerprints! Don't mark them, arrgh! you idiot that label's 0.00003 degrees crooked!) Then work out the postage dependent on size and weight... oh, oh, oh, sometimes we got to stock the shelves for 'pick-ups'.

On a truly special day we got to unpack the books from pallets and match them with the orders, (ohhhh I'm trembling with excitement... tie me down!). The money was minimum wage. My job was basic and mundane, and any helpful suggestions or creativity shown by me, were treated with disdain, if acknowledged at all. Fair enough, I only had twenty years of broad business and sales experience, no useful input at all.

But glory to God, in the midst of this, there was a ray of divine sunshine. The most wonderful co-worker in the WORLD! Anne, you saved my sanity and possibly my life – you are amazing! ☺ We had the best discussions about all sorts of subjects, we laughed (a lot) and cried together. You even managed to stop me from punching out that completely arrogant d-head of a boss! I could NEVER see how either you or Michael, (the other boss, Mr smooth-savvy-entreprenurial-totally-onto-it guy, but as emotionally sensitive and as demonstrative as a rock) could stand him, never mind work with him! s-i-g-h … still a bit of emotion there for me huh.

Unfortunately, it wasn't just at the job that I was feeling unappreciated and rejected. We had left New Zealand, sold everything, and taken a leap of faith to go and live in France. I was mentally, emotionally, financially and spiritually ready for a life in France. I knew it would be tough, and there would be challenges and hardships, but I loved Paris and the French. Also, I felt called, the sacrifices we were making and would make, had meaning and purpose there.

The French celebrated individuality, they celebrated variety, they had passion, they loved to talk ideas, philosophy and religion even if they didn't agree with you. The French like the Irish (me) didn't mind if you didn't agree, you could still be best friends and disagree on just about everything. Denmark was different, almost a cultural opposite; rules and structure were important and conformity paramount. You did not question, especially if you were a foreigner. In general, 'foreigners' are not liked or wanted in THEIR country, and if you had the temerity to live there, then you'd better bloody well fit in. You must follow the rules, no exceptions, don't question or dare to step outside of the box, just do as the state and society tells you. Accept it, do not resist, we do know better than you – we are Danish. Please don't react, don't get worked up about anything, its ok, we ignore everyone else too, you're not special. Yes, the grey trousers look best, maybe black or white. What are you screaming for, please quieten down, it's embarrassing.

Denmark was the first place where I felt demeaned, disrespected, disregarded, and constantly in the wrong. I was also 'grieving' the whole loss of vision, Paris was dead and buried, I felt at a loss within myself. When you combine those things with a menial job which was totally doing my head in... well there had to be an explosion somewhere, right?

It happened near the end of a crappy day; I was using the manual hoist to take the left over pallets and packing boxes down to the bins. When I got to the lift, this other dude was just getting in with some delivery boxes... he saw me, but pressed the door closed anyway (though there was plenty of room) huh... cheers jerk... I waited and waited, after about five minutes I jogged down the stairs to see what was going on... and here was this guy having a conversation on the phone with the lift doors blocked open and its empty inside!

Oi mate, don't worry, you're obviously the only one on the planet, they made the lift just for you to use. He saw me again as he'd hung up, but no apology, not even a little nod of acknowledgement – nothing. Hopping in the lift I unlocked the doors and went up and got my hoist. I came down, just barely managed to squeeze past his truck which was blocking the front entrance and round to the bins. After unloading I headed back; suddenly this truck roars round the corner, just about takes me out (though it's in a whole empty car park) and he blasts the horn at me. Well, well, enough is enough aye, not wanting to get too angry, but desiring to communicate my displeasure I give him the finger, he deserved that and more, pillock! Good riddance, dickhead! But no! He slams on the brakes and leaps out of the truck, comes storming towards me shouting and spitting like a smacked snake.....

Important Southern Hemisphere cultural note: If you pull this stunt down under, you'll better be ready, because he crossed the line, now it's ALL on!

"the talkin is over - it's fightin time"

Important European cultural note: Fight, do you mean, like actually hit someone, how barbaric! someone might get hurt! Let's just shout a bit at each other, gesticulate wildly, but never fight – we're not savages!

You can see what's coming can't you.

As he's storming towards me; the adrenaline is pumping, but I am SO READY for this, he's got no idea how much I'm relishing a good fight, I am going to smear him! He's bigger than me, but flabby and I am laser focused.

I walk towards him, don't say a word, grab him by the collar and body slam him against the side of the truck. With a snarl, I draw back my fist to smash him, when two things happen at once; he suddenly realises he's taken a mouth to a fist fight with a foreigner and secondly, I see how scared he is.

Putting his arm up to protect his head, he cringes, (WTF!) and whimpers (in English, no less)

"No, No, don't hurt me! Don't hurt me!"

Baffled by his sudden change in attitude and frankly whimpy reaction, reluctantly I let him go after pushing him against the truck again. I am telling him colourfully, how he is rather inconsiderate and nearly ran me over. Still pleading with me and looking like he's about to piss his pants, he stumbles off to the front of the cab where he locks himself in. (Grow a pair dude!) I'm still angry and shout at him hiding in the cab, telling him to man up and come out and finish what he started, but I'm confused too, didn't he want to fight? He'd jumped out of the cab and come storming towards me, shouting and cursing, hadn't he? I'd been ready to dodge the first roundhouse. Didn't you guys come from Vikings? I couldn't believe how much of a pussy he was.

I was angry at him, but also a little guilty (some Christian witness I was). I was so ready to go all fight club, it had felt good to slam him up against the truck. It had taken considerable will power not to smash him, but the fear in his eyes had finally penetrated my anger and stopped me.

Anyway, Mr Bravery finally rolls his window down a fraction and tells me he's going to call the police and charge me with assault, they'll be here in about fifteen minutes. I tell him, he'd been the one coming at me and why didn't he man up and come down and talk to me about it. He said I was crazy, (probably not far wrong) and that I'd assault him again, (again, possible), so he was going to wait in his cab till the cops came. I'd been in Denmark long enough to know that any Danish cop would be on the locals' side and would throw the book at some bloody foreigner who had the nerve to marry one of theirs.

Not really knowing what else to do, I went back up to work and explained what had happened to Michael, not holding anything back. I explained that I had been finding it difficult to adjust to Denmark and the guy had just hit all the right buttons and I'd lost it.

I apologised to Michael and said sorry for possibly tarnishing his companies name, and not acting very Christian like. Michael went down to talk to him and came back up about thirty minutes later and told me that it was all ok, he'd talked to the guy and also to his boss and had straitened it all out.

Michael rose considerably in my estimation that afternoon; I saw a side of him I hadn't known existed before, he was unusually compassionate and non-judgmental with me and he had handled the driver and his boss perfectly.

When he came back up to the office, he told me he was glad I hadn't done anything more to the driver, as in Denmark the company the person works for, is the one who has to pay all the medical bills, salary and damages! I was mortified, here was I this supposed "Godly" missionary, angrily lashing out like some crazy criminal and not knowing I could have cost David 100,000's of Kroner, all because he'd been kind enough to give a friends' brother in law a job! Not cool Rich, not cool. I knew I needed to take some time off and get my head sorted before I repaid his kindness with some other foolishness. The next day, I told Michael it would be best if I finished up at the end of the following week. You know what, he agreed.

Michael impressed me again in that following week, I felt awful that I had come so close to causing a disaster. I tried to explain why it had happened and some of the stuff I was going through. He listened and said not to worry about it – he even offered to pay for a psychologist for me, impressive dude. What's more, a few months later, David arranged and paid for the re-delivery to Copenhagen of our stuff which had been sent to Paris from New Zealand, wow, more impressive.

Truth be told I was already seeing a psychologist. I knew I wasn't "feeling great" and I was getting depressed and drinking too much, so we'd looked around to try and find someone to help. I'd ended up with a nice guy called Philip, not too far from where I lived in Copenhagen. My sessions with him were extremely effective at digging stuff up, some of which I had totally purged from my mind. However, no offence to Philip he was next to useless in helping me deal with what came up. For goodness sake he was saying I should roll a towel up like a sausage and beat the floor with it. Seriously!? How is that ever going to help a man with a modicum of testosterone and shit loads of anger and frustration? Giving the floor a whippin' with a rolled-up towel, oh please! It was all so PC, emasculated Danish. I wanted to scream and go all "Fight Club", now THAT would help.

ROOT OF THE PROBLEM

My problems had started when I was young; I was born and raised in Northern Ireland in the late 60's early 70's. If you know your history, you'll realise that they were crazy, violent, and troubled times in Ireland. When I was eight, God spoke to my father and told him to take the family and leave Northern Ireland, quickly. There had already been three attempts on his life in the previous year, so a scant four weeks later we arrived in Auckland, New Zealand. We knew no-one and had no clue about what NZ was like, all Dad knew was that it looked like the best place in the British commonwealth to go farming.

Though I knew it was for the best that we left Ireland, I was heart-broken, made worse by the suddenness of it all. I had great relationships with my grandparents, and I knew I might never see them again, (I didn't). Then began a new life in Hamilton, New Zealand. For me with my strong Irish accent and completely different worldview, life was "challenging". I didn't even last a day at the first school I went to. The school was in the country and I was the only pakeha boy there, and a foreigner, so Hola Señor Piñata. In the end the teachers called my parents and asked them to take me away for fear that it would go too far.

The next school was better, Frankton Primary, I lasted three days. In the early 1970's there was no political correctness and immigrants were still rare. Three Maori boys were not going to tolerate some foreign boy in their back yard. The first morning, literally as I was walking in the school gate, I commenced my "speech therapy" sessions.

"Hey bro – you talk funny, you're not gonna talk funny like that anymore, Ae"

BAM! BAM! Two punches to the face ended lesson one. They were generous with their tuition; three sessions a day, morning, lunchtime (with my lunch as payment) and just after school.

Then I was sent to Melville Primary. Phew, most of the immigrants went there, so my school life settled down a little. Slowly I began to adapt and make friends, they were immigrant's too (a Chinese and a Fijian) and we were all mad about this new thing called peanut butter on toast. It was delicious.

Then one fateful day, three months later we had some visitors come to see my parents at our dairy farm. I was in fine form that day and was tearing around as 8-year old boys do! Mum exasperated at my high jinx, (though she recalls it as a concern for my education) asked the visitors which school their son went too. They said St Peters private school, just outside Cambridge, it was a boarding school.

We visited the school, Mum and Dad prayed about it and that was that – I was enrolled. Heee-ya... I was devastated and distraught, how could they abandon me at a boarding school? My parents and my sister were the only security and connection from Ireland and I wouldn't even have them. This was the root of much of my anguish in later years. I had been taken away from all other friends and loving family in Ireland. Now my only security and connection, my family, was ditching me at a boarding school. Seriously?

I didn't understand why I wasn't there for the week, then home for the weekend. This was totally do-able, as they lived nearby. No, it was boarding full time, for the whole term. They'd come every few weeks on Sunday afternoons for a couple of hours, to have lunch with me in the school grounds. As you can imagine, as I was the youngest at the school, it was brutal, boys are cruel, it's survival of the fittest.

One of my strongest memories from that time, which I had suppressed for many years, is running after my parent's car as it drove off out of the school grounds. I was chasing their car crying and screaming, totally distraught. I was calling out and pleading with them to stop and take me home with them...and they just drove away... didn't even acknowledge me. (even my sister, not too fond of me at the time, remembers it well, she says it was one of the few times she truly felt sorry for me).

Anyway, I'd never dealt properly with any of this, so on top of the constant rejection I felt in Denmark and the shattering of the French vision, I was in a deep dark hole. Talking it through with the psychologist was fine, but the pain was raw and deep and bashing the floor with a towel was never going to cut it. Praise God there was a glimmer of hope at the bottom of that dark well, Louise and I had come across a Christian Inner Healing therapy; "Theophostic Ministries".

There were some practitioners in a YWAM base in Restenas, Sweden. By this time in October 2007 I was falling apart, I was desperate, so I booked myself in there, the day after I'd be returning from Paris.

Yes! I was going back to Paris, albeit it briefly. My best friend, had shouted me tickets to the final of the Rugby World Cup, Yee-ha! We hoped to see the All Blacks VS ? in the final, unfortunately, France and inexperience put paid to that, the weekend before we left. Never mind, it was still all arranged, and I was still going to Paris for the week, awesome right. Well, no; my apologies Alf, I was such a mess and inside my head I was in hell. I've never felt so anguished and tormented in my life and I just couldn't deal with it. The sessions with the psychologist had only re-opened old wounds and they had gone septic.

A weakness of mine is drinking. Ever since I'd left home, I'd drink a fair bit, mostly it wasn't too bad, but every few months I'd overdo it and get hammered. At university I was a pretty social guy and went out most weekends and every so often I'd get tanked. My resulting behaviour depended on how drunk I got, though mostly it wasn't awful – If I really tied one on, I wasn't giggly, happy or sleepy but morose and depressed. As I got older it was much worse, and now I was a belligerent drunk. When I had been in Paris the first time, it had happened every few months, though I was careful to be by myself. A grumpy, drunk missionary guy isn't the best of looks.

Now years later, since we'd settled in Denmark, I'd been finding myself drinking a lot more and nearly every night. It helped me dull the pain, but it was taking more and more to dull the pain and was getting out of hand.

That week in Paris without Louise's constraining influence I went crazy twice. The last time, I was in so much mental anguish that Alf's tolerance finally evaporated, and we fought, he wrestled me to the ground and tried to calm me down. Thanks Alf, for not giving up on me that night I was a complete idiot. I was in so much pain, the feelings of abandonment took over, I truly felt like I was losing my mind. Alf (the angel) finally got us back to the apartment and the following day we went our separate ways. He back to New Zealand and me back to Denmark. One thing that night made abundantly clear, If I didn't get help soon, I'd totally lose it and I would lose my wife, my beautiful family, and possibly my life.

When I arrived back from Paris, it was only for one night and I managed to hold it together. The next day I set off to Restenas in Sweden. I was falling apart at the seams, unravelling, I needed a miracle. I arrived in Restanas in the early afternoon, where I found Laura and her mother waiting for me. We decided that if I was up for it, we'd get straight into it.

The principle of Theophostic ministry is that the 'councillors' act as facilitators, basically asking questions, guiding you to where the problems lie. The premise is we all have these persistent lies we believe and which the enemy uses to gain access to our lives. The facilitator asks questions to identify the places these lies have entered your life. Then you ask Jesus to bring truth into the situation and BOOM the lie is gone!

Honestly, I didn't know if it would work, or even how it would work; but after spending three hours talking with Laura and her mum I felt re-born. An enormous weight had been taken off my soul, I felt liberated, like I could fly. I had an incredible feeling of lightness and freedom, walking around the YWAM base I felt if i flapped my arms or ran down a hill I'd take off. Most of the darkness and depression had left, I was in a place of peace. To consolidate the amazing transformation we had another session the next morning before I left, but it was hardly necessary, I was a new person. The torment and the anguish were gone! Praise the Lord!

I was late arriving home and Louise was quite upset at me – but I was in a state of bliss – even Louise could see the dramatic change, I was at peace.

The Theophostic prayer radically changed me, I'm not exaggerating to say it saved my life. I'd like to say that everything from there on was rosy and wonderful, but life is a little more complex than that. It was definitely a turn in the road, dealing with some deep-rooted lies and giving me fresh hope and life.

LIFE IN DENMARK CONTINUES

I was still grieving over France not happening, but decided that God could use me in Denmark, even though I was struggling. As I didn't have a job, I set out on a campaign to try and do some "prophetic evangelism" or being bold and asking people if I could pray for them. I'd cycle around Copenhagen and when I felt there was a hint of an opportunity, I'd go for it. Unfortunately, it didn't seem to work; no-one got obviously healed and no one was any more inclined to become a Christian. Some of the conversations were interesting though, and I trust God some seeds were planted.

Another miracle shortly after that; I got a job working for an international PC security company. They hired me to ring international clients and sell their security software. I'm not usually the number 1 sales person, but I have plenty of experience and consistently exceed my targets, but not there - almost no sales. NOTHING I did made the least bit of difference, even my managers were amazed, they piggy backed on the calls, checked my proposals, listened in on my sales presentations, they couldn't get it either. People all around me were making regular sales; but not me – I was doing everything right, saying the right stuff but no deals… huh? (I call it a "negative" miracle). I have no idea why God had me there as part of the company for only three or four months. He easily could have answered my prayers for sales in an instant, but he didn't. He knew I'd need another major dose of his "peace" before that final fateful week; so surprise, surprise, I ended up for a further weekend in Restenas, dealing with more stuff, (including things rising out of my 'failure' at the job).

I arrived back after the weekend in Restenas in a wonderful state of peace. Everything was ok, God was in control, despite what it looked like. I am 100% certain that if I hadn't had that weekend at Restenas, I would have punched out my Sales Manager that Monday.

He was totally on my case the whole day (frustration driven I think), he kept making disparaging comments and giving me snark. He knew I was doing the work, he knew I was putting in the hours, he'd heard me innumerable times and thought it was good, but nobody knew why I was bombing. He'd even told me I should lie to get the business and went ahead and showed me how it was done on a call – it worked – I'd heard him do it many times before, but I couldn't do that, sorry. You can fire my ass, but I'm not betraying my principles.

Long story short, I got called into the HR manager's office late that Monday afternoon and both he and the sales manager were there. They highlighted that I'd been there three months, they had used considerable 'resources' training me and I had sold almost zip, so what should they do about it? I was to come up with some ideas and a plan for the following day. Ahh OK…

The following day I suggested a sideways move into marketing and identified several areas I could help in and outlined a plan. The Sales manager gave me the steely look and said. No – sorry Richard, we've decided to let you go. As everything was 'security to paranoid' levels, I had to leave immediately, security guard with you to gather any personal things. Then BOOM you're out and cycling home a bit dazed, wondering what the heck just happened and how fast it had all been.

Amazingly and miraculously, I was totally at peace, knowing that God was somehow, strangely in it all. Now many years later, I'm still unsure why I worked there for only three months. Maybe it was about a friendship I made with Danish / Hungarian I met there; a guy who was working in IT. We've always got on really well and are still good friends, so maybe he's the reason. Hmmm… whatever it was - it was a weird and stressful three months.

It was now July 2008 and Praise God for Danish summer, the light is golden and there's a beauty and ease about life in Denmark. People are optimistic and there's hope drifting in the air. Oliver was now a year old and was a true delight, he was the happiest, easiest baby I'd ever known. Arianna was fitting into a new, much better, local kindergarten and Isabella would soon be going too.

We had almost no money, though Louisa was getting some help from the system to support the kids. I was applying for different jobs left, right and centre to no avail. I even went and saw a guy from a recruitment company to figure out what I was doing wrong; he said I was doing nothing wrong. He was very impressed with my CV and its presentation and was surprised himself that I hadn't been able to get a job yet. (I was getting pretty fed up with these 'negative' miracles). Bear in mind this was late 2008 and Europe was feeling the pinch of the Global Financial Crisis, there were no jobs for Danes, never mind foreigners.

Then in August, I met Torsten through his wife Gitte who went along to Vineyard. Torsten and I got on like a house on fire – he was very un-Danish. Extroverted, colourful, loud, showed his emotions, and was not averse to tooting his own horn. He was quite the exception in Denmark; I loved him.

At the time Torsten was the Managing Director of a large brewery in Germany, so each week he'd be away in Bamberg, Bavaria and only get back on the weekends, so I didn't see him often. A month or so after we'd met, Torsten rang me up and said he'd like me to work as a contractor for him. He'd pay expenses as they occurred, but I'd get properly paid only after the job was done. Money wise it wasn't very helpful, but it was great for my confidence and my head space. He wanted some help with photography, marketing and editing / writing business proposals in English. He'd been instructed by his investors that he needed to find a buyer for the brewery as they wanted to get out.

I did some short work for him from home, mostly turning his Danglish proposals into English (though he was pretty good). I also prepared some English power point presentations and reviewed some documents. Then Torsten said he had serious investors from Prague and wanted me to come with him to Bamberg, Germany to put together the proposal. Being with Torsten was a tonic for me, he trusted me and gave me lots of jobs to do and was happy with the results. He certainly helped me gain back a little of my shattered confidence. After we got back Torsten asked me to edit the proposal for the investors from Czechoslovakia and to help with other documentation, as they looked like the best and most likely buyers for the brewery. To my surprise and delight he asked me to go to Prague with him for the discussions and negotiations with their team. As always with Torsten it was a full on few days. But we did manage to get out for a few hours and do the tourist thing, Prague is beautiful, very picturesque. Best news of all was that they eventually agreed on terms and bought out the brewery, though that meant that Torsten himself was out of a job.

In true "Torsten" style, it was a brief interlude before he was involved with another project that needed investors and someone to drive it. He asked me to work with him, we got on really well, he valued my varied skillset and most importantly, he trusted me.

On the face of it this sounded perfect and I was keen to leap in, but Louisa had a few misgivings about Torsten, so I thought I'd better take some time aside and pray and fast about it before making a decision. After a few days I was a little surprised that It was a clear "no" from God. This was not the right thing for me to be doing even though it looked like an amazing opportunity. I told Torsten as gently as I could that though I really, really appreciated the offer, I felt it was the wrong thing for me to do – in a God sense. Torsten and I had talked many times about God. He knew that my relationship with God and obedience to him was paramount to me, so he sort-of understood, though it did put a dent in our friendship for a while.

He and Gitte thought I was using "God" as an excuse for 'self-sabotage'. I could see how it looked from his perspective and could agree a little, but I was convinced that God had said a firm no. It was an incredibly hard decision. Torsten had been great to me, we worked well together and I wanted to take up his offer. I could see I had hurt Torsten and he felt I had rebuffed his generosity, I could understand how that must have looked like, unfortunately, I believed God had given me a firm no, so no, it was.

CHURCH IN DENMARK

Ahh Richard, at last, a positive about Denmark. Surely church must have been great, right? They had been very supportive of the plans to set up a Vineyard in Paris, like a daughter church. Sadly, it was not turning out as I'd hoped or expected. The home group that we went to, (well mostly Louisa) didn't want it to get "too personal", I kid you not, the leader specifically said that. I went to church occasionally still, but there was no real connection with the people there or seeming concern. As for my Danish male friends (excepting Torsten) I discovered something; they don't do deep. Do 'church', have a coffee, have a beer, maybe a meal, but don't open up at all, don't get intimate – that shit don't go down. If you're struggling, or you go deep, there's an awkward embarrassed silence, like someone dropped a nasty fart. They just didn't know what to say or do.

Classic example; I had gone back to church one Sunday and what I thought was a good friend of mine, came up to me and asked me how it was going. I asked, do you really want to know? (you've got to check, right) Yes, he said, so I told him that honestly, it was "shitty" - I was barely holding it together, I was badly depressed and had even contemplated suicide. He looked at me, his face solemn and said "oh, OK…" looked awkward for a second or two, then turned around and walked off… really; seriously; yo dude, W.T.F?!

I'd noticed it with other male Danish friends as well, they were great guys and were fun to be with, but take your heart out and put it on the table and the shutters came down. They couldn't or wouldn't deal with it. They wouldn't look at you, they'd be really awkward, then disappear first chance they had, I didn't understand at all. Still don't, maybe one of you Danes could enlighten me. I suspect it's a cultural thing, was I too much, too transparent. I'm sure they wanted to help, just had no idea how.

This resulted in me feeling truly isolated and I had no one in Denmark to turn to, even Louisa. She changed when she was in Denmark and with her family, she became Louisa Toft again. For her Denmark and the Danish was 'normal' she could fit in – it wasn't a big deal for her, in fact it was the life and lifestyle she was used to. I knew it was incredibly difficult for her to be married to me, she didn't really 'get' what I was about, and agreed more with her family and their position. I needed to get my act together, work hard, do the right, approved of thing, blend in, and stop rocking the boat!

By now it was 2009 and the year started off with two glimmers of hope; first I had completely stopped drinking and secondly, I'd discovered the gym.

I'd stopped drinking as it was becoming more frequent again, too much, too often, and it was putting a real strain on our marriage. Looking back, I really didn't get how bad it was with me, it was a constant worry and fear for Louise. What 'Richard' would it be tonight, would I be aggressive and argumentative or depressed, sullen and withdrawn. New Years eve 2009 I'd had a tad too much and whilst I wasn't raucous or going wild, I'd fallen asleep in my arms on the table and Isabella had come up to me and put a blanket over me. Obviously, Louisa was embarrassed, I mean this was with her family after all. I found out later one of her family members told Louise she should just leave me. I was obviously a train wreck they didn't need to be part of.

To give you some context; I'd been asked to one of the family's places about 6 months before, where two of Louisa's siblings met me and proceeded to tell me I needed to get my act together. I should realise that my (faith based) approach was wrong and I needed to make an effort to do things the "Danish" way, (If it's not happening - make it happen). The unspoken narrative was that I must change, be somebody, do something that was acceptable and palatable to be associated with. Do not be this mad Irish / Kiwi bloke who was opinionated and passionate, a little too large for life, impulsive, unpredictable and frankly a mess. As you can imagine that went down like a rat sandwich. I was shocked and angry. Not trusting myself to say anything as I was close to losing it, I'd quickly left the apartment. Better to leave them surprised by my hasty and rude departure than give them a piece of my mind, especially as I was livid. Staying and unloading would not have been a wise choice and would have burned rather than mended already shaky bridges.

Surprisingly giving up drinking was much easier than I'd thought. As an alternative to vent my myriad of frustrations I started going to the gym. Wow! That was awesome! I could pound my body and clear my head in an acceptable manner. It had a flow on effect too, I started to gain some confidence back and felt a lot healthier in myself, more optimistic about life.

NORTHERN IRELAND, AN OPTION?

Meanwhile, Geoff my cousin in Enniskillen, Northern Ireland was a GP and part of a practice – he asked me if I'd consider being their "Practice Manager" i.e. handle all the business aspects of the practice. I said sure, but I'd have to pray about it and we'd come over and "suss" it out, as we'd need to see if Louisa and the kids would be ok with moving there too.

Both Louise and I were pretty stressed by this time, as we had no money left, and I was really struggling to keep it together. Praise God, I'd stopped drinking and was going to the gym, otherwise I think the wheels would have fallen off. Thankfully, Geoff helped us with the fares. As a family we were finding it difficult as Arianna was now having a tough time at kindergarten and Isabella wasn't thriving there either. I was a stay at home Dad as Louise now had a part time job. I was still looking for a job without success. I was thinking more and more that Denmark and I were badly incompatible, so maybe a sideways move to Northern Ireland would help.

We were all tired when we finally got to Geoff's place, it had been a pretty long trip for the kids as we'd flown into Dublin, four hours away by car. Geoff had dropped us off and had headed off to Donegal where Sarah-Claire and the family were staying. We had an early night, tucked the kids in their beds and talked for a while, then Louisa went to bed (we were sleeping in the "loft"). I decided to read for a bit before turning in.

Ten minutes later the quiet night was shattered by screaming and Louisa came flying down out of the loft, crying and screaming hysterically. I was badly worried, what on earth had gone wrong. I held her and asked what the matter was, she was crying and slumped on the couch saying she just couldn't take any more, she was totally distraught. After she calmed down a little, she told me there was something up there in the loft that had got caught in her hair and had totally freaked her out. I went upstairs, wondering what on earth it was – a bird? I had a good look around and discovered the culprit – a bat. No wonder she freaked out. It made creepy mouse / rat like squealing noises as it flew around. Louisa hates mice! Like really hates them, so a flying one was a nightmare made real. I let it out the window and went down to see if Louisa was ok, she was still pretty upset but was in a much better place. She slept downstairs that night.

That opening night meant that the rest of the visit to Ireland had to be pretty exceptional for us to consider moving there. The schools seemed fine, and the work, and work environment seemed good as well. However, after a few days I knew I did not want to live in Northern Ireland, unless God specifically and (very) clearly told me.

The thing that got me, happened two days after we arrived, I went for a bike downtown Enniskillen, unbeknown to me this was the season of marches for the "Orangemen" and downtown that day they were preparing to do a march. As I watched them strut and bolster in their uniforms and robes, I was horrified and honestly a little scared. The hatred, pride and arrogance rolled off them in waves. The way they conducted themselves shouted "blood" for any who would dare oppose them. Coming from New Zealand and Denmark I was shocked, public expressions of hatred and violence are rare there. Unfortunately, this experience was reinforced several times in our fortnights stay there, though it wasn't always the Orange order. One time when we were travelling by car through a republican area, the hatred and hostility were thick enough to slice. I quickly realised I couldn't deal with such a high level of hatred, hostility and 'murder'. I was also surprised that I picked it up so quickly. I suspect it was God letting me know what the environment was like.

I later learned that those particular few weeks in summer are the "period" where all the marches and hostilities generally occur, so no surprise that tensions were heightened, and the spiritual and emotional moods were so negative. Understandably, we decided we were not meant to live in Northern Ireland. We did have a great time with relatives and had a chance to catch up with my mother's side of the family which was fantastic. I even met my mother's older sister, Aunt Eunice for the first time. We had such a warm welcome from all my cousins, it felt like coming home. With relatives it was wonderful and I could see us doing well there as a family, but the initial night and the heavy atmosphere meant we needed a clear, as in blindingly obvious, sign from God. That didn't happen, so whilst we'd had a much needed break we decided that Northern Ireland wasn't what God had in mind for us.

BACK IN DENMARK

In Denmark we were wondering what to do now, how were we going to survive?

We were living on 'fumes', all the money we'd put aside for Paris was long gone, Denmark was expensive. As I hadn't had a sniff of a 'real' job, Louisa applied to Johannasskole in Hillerød to see if she could get a teaching job. She got the job, working twenty-seven hours a week, ya-hoo! Though she was working a little over "half time" Louisa was still up at 5.30am and returning late in the afternoon. I was now Mr House Hubby looking after the kids; which fortunately wasn't too bad as Arianna and Isabella went to a local kindergarten and Oliver went to the same day care for a few hours.

While the money was a lot better with Louisa working – I wasn't enthralled with my new role and didn't feel like I was any 'good' at it either.

I did the shopping (ok fine) the cooking (ok fine) cleaning (yuk!) and looking after the kids, (hmmm I'm not good at that when I'm struggling).

On top of this I felt tremendously guilty for not having Oliver and Isabella at 'home' during the day as they were younger, but truth be told I couldn't have coped.

It helped that they all went to the same place and that it was one of the better places around with good care givers. Isabella was enjoying it and seemed to be having fun. Of course, Oliver had one of the carers totally bananas about him, showering him with love and affection.

I consoled myself with the fact that it was only for a few hours and better for them than hanging out with their deeply depressed Dad!

Yes, it was official, a phycologist said I was suffering from clinical depression, severe even. Same could be said of my spiritual life, I tried to read the Bible and pray, but there was so much confusion and pain I didn't know what to do.

Generally speaking this period of time was an improvement over the previous years, though I was finding it harder to deal with living in Denmark and honestly felt the distance between Louise and I was becoming greater.

On top of this was the stress of no money, we were barely making ends meet. In February 2009 the financial pressure became too much and we left the flat in Copenhagen. Interestingly a month after we left the apartment which was the bottom story in a house, the home was condemned and evacuated as there was too much toxic mould in the walls! No wonder Isabella had been constantly sniffly and under the weather for two years.

HILLERØD

We went to live with Mr & Mrs Toft, Louisa's parents in Hillerød. The idea was that we'd save money on Copenhagen rent and Louisa's parents were literally up the road from the school Louisa worked at. From Louisa's parents place, we'd look for an apartment or house in Hillerød or the surrounding districts. It'd be much easier for Louisa to travel to school and Hillerød was much cheaper both for rent and for transport. Besides Hillerød and the surrounds were quite beautiful with plenty of lakes and forest. We looked and we looked, in both Hillerød and the surrounding areas, but no luck. We even had the inside track on 2 places, but at the last minute when hope was rising, bam! The door would slam on us again. Huh?

While Louisa was working, I was applying for jobs in the area and sending feelers out for jobs in New Zealand. To give you an example, I had a friend who had a 20-30 hour a week cleaning job at a church and old peoples home. He called me and said that he had to stop work, would I like to take over his job? Yes please! He said it shouldn't be an issue, he'd been there for years and they trusted him, so his recommendation would likely be a 'shoe in'. Ahhh not really, they told him they were not going to replace him, as things had got tighter financially.

After a month at Louisa's parents, and having no luck with alternative accommodation, we needed to make a decision about what we were going to do. After praying, we decided, all the shut doors must mean we should go back to New Zealand. Within myself, I was certain the signs were pointing that way, and we had given God full opportunity to open the doors for us in Hillerød. It was especially difficult for Louisa, as she wanted to stay close to her family and there was "pressure" on her to stay.

In the end, it was blindingly obvious I wasn't getting a job anytime soon and secondly, we weren't getting an apartment anytime soon either. We prayed and asked God to confirm it. Fortunately we both felt it was the right time to return to New Zealand. Once the decision was made, it became easier as we could now enjoy the last six weeks in Denmark. Understandably, Mrs Toft was greatly disappointed, which made life at their place more tense. Whether it was true or not, I had the impression they weren't happy, the maverick, crazy, Irishman was taking their daughter and grandkids off again! Woohoo, no guilt or anything.

It was the start of a glorious summer in Denmark and we'd been given a house by the beach to get away for a few days as a family. During this period I was interviewed for a "Business Coach" job back in New Zealand. It seemed a fantastic job, paid well, and was even based in Hamilton. On Skype, they were positive and subsequent emails seemed to suggest that I pretty much "had" the job already. When I arrived back, I just needed to go see them and they'd slot me into the appropriate industry and position. Fantastic. The doors seemed to be opening.

We enjoyed the summer including the most amazing swarm of ladybugs I have ever witnessed in my life – there were MILLIONS of ladybirds at a beach in North Zeeland. I didn't even know you could get that many ladybirds in one place, it was freakish in a wonderful way. I was literally covered with hundreds of ladybirds. They were flying around so thickly there was a haze in the air!

The time quickly came for us to leave; which was good, as things were tense between me and some of the family. I understood where they were coming from but we (particularly me) were in a bad way emotionally. I felt for us to remain together as a family we needed to go back to NZ.

RETURN TO NEW ZEALAND

August 22nd we arrived back in NZ, first obstacle was in the airport. Oliver had only a Danish passport, so wasn't supposed to be allowed in. Secondly, despite a multi-entry visa and a permanent residents visa ... Louisa wasn't allowed in either. Apparently, the permanent visa automatically expires when you leave the country and you need a re-entrant's visa. You're kidding right? Me, the New Zealand citizen, was not happy being delayed by officious customs for 3 hours after a 35 hour journey!

We finally got through, and my sister took us back to her house in Hamilton. The idea was for us to stay with them till we had our own place, in either Cambridge or Hamilton.

First up was my final interview with the coaching company, so bright eyed and bushy tailed I turned up there two days later. To my surprise, there was a lot more riding on this interview than I had been told. It was with the CEO to see if I'd fit in with everyone else and contribute to the firm. OK, that should be fine, right? Have you ever had that situation when you walk into a room and meet someone and you KNOW it's down the toilet before it's even started. The moment I walked in, I KNEW I was never going to work there. Sometimes you just clash with someone and know it straight away. Yup, I felt like punching him in the face almost from the get go, he was an insufferable, pretentious, arrogant little sausage. Imagine how he felt about me! The result of the interview was forgone.

Time to apply for other jobs, which I had been doing, but now I really swung into it. All to NO avail. Oh come on! Maybe it was because I was now over 40 so "undesirable". Even basic part time jobs were eluding me, with no other option, I applied for the dole; awesome, super... first time in my life. VERY humbling.

I must say when we arrived back in New Zealand we were overwhelmed with people's kindness. The cell group we'd been a part of and the church gave us a car. Amazing! No way we could have afforded one, we were already in debt. Then the church put on a dinner for us (I was really struggling to put on a social / happy face) and they gave us the proceeds. On top of that several people generously gave us furniture and bits and pieces to set up house. Yes! We'd finally found one, 6 weeks after arriving back, we moved into our current address – with many sighs of relief all round.

Though I did my best to present the best front I could; I was a broken man and still seriously depressed. I felt like I'd barely escaped from Denmark with my sanity, had we stayed there, I believe Louise and I would have separated. Point in case, a good friend of mine in Denmark, a guy from Texas; showed how bad it could get. He couldn't handle the Danish culture and how it held him and all other foreigners in contempt. He started to drink more and he slowly withdrew from his wife and daughter and his life fell apart. Last I heard from him he'd been kicked out of Denmark and was shacked up with a Norwegian girl from a mental institution, on a boat in Norway. Amazingly, even though they were both alcoholics, he'd got her pregnant. I tried to get in contact with him afterwards, as I heard he'd been sent back to the States, but all the calls went unanswered and I don't know where he is now, the poor bastard. Tex, if you're out there and you ever read this; God loves you and so do I. Know that God has his hand on your life so please get in touch with him and me too!

It was good to be back in New Zealand and people had shown us such kindness, but I was struggling in every way. We had taken huge steps of faith; we had put it all on the line, why had we crashed and burned so badly? I was so incredibly angry at God and I'd lost a lot of my confidence, normal optimism, and social ability. Fortunately, I still wasn't drinking or that would have been a total disaster. (Hmmm, don't worry that came soon enough). Honestly, it was my beautiful children that kept me in the world those days. Without them, I don't know if I'd still be around, I was in a deep dark place and didn't know what to do to stay sane and alive. My faith had taken a hammering and my hope for the future was all but extinguished.

THE SEARCH FOR WORK

It was strange to fit back into New Zealand again, especially as no job, meant money was always tight. We made it through the first few months on the generosity of friends and a burgeoning overdraft! I applied for many jobs but wasn't rung back, never mind an interview. Trying to stay positive, I was doing a reasonable amount of exercise and had recently come across this amazing thing called Kettlebells. The moment I found out about them I was hooked, the perfect "minimum effective dose" (MED, thank you Tim Ferriss) for exercise. Then one day while I was out on a run, I realised that I really loved the whole exercise deal and helping people – so why not be a personal trainer. By now I was proficient at Kettlebells and was teaching some others privately and at a local gym. I enrolled as a full-time student and started to work as an exercise consultant (ie. Dogs body) at another local gym.

Being a student again was wonderful, I love learning and it was fascinating to learn how our bodies function. As Sir Isaac Newton once observed; you only need to look at your thumb to realise there must be a creator, for we are fearfully and wonderfully made. We are brilliantly complex, biological machines. Take the Krebs cycle for instance, (which is only one small part of how our body converts food to energy for our muscles). It is an incredibly complex series of chemical reactions involving numerous molecules and a myriad of enzymes. Check it out on you tube, it'll amaze you! It boggles my mind what a huge amount of faith it takes to believe all that beauty and complexity came from evolution.

My routine was to go to "school" some days and the weekends; then during the week I'd work 4 hours a day at the gym and do some kettlebell or bootcamp classes on top of that.

Over the next few years I worked at various gyms, mostly doing contract Kettlebell classes and bootcamps. I was about to sign up for a Hamilton gym as their in-house Personal Trainer, but that morning I got a crazy injury while doing pull ups. I pulled some nerves or did something to my back, it was a little unclear what exactly happened. The result was that my whole back was in constant muscle spasms and cramps, it was agonising for a few days till the Doctor tried 'epileptic' medication which basically knocked me out for 18 hours! When I woke up, it was mostly gone and after another week or so it had settled down. Meanwhile I had not been able to work at all, no PT, no classes, I could hardly get out of bed for the first week, never mind help people with exercise. It was then I realised, if you're in the exercise game and you're injured - you're broke.

What should I say about this four years in my life? I had a number of jobs mostly self- employed, but I was limping from contract to contract instead of a full time job that paid well and was consistent. I applied for several sales orientated and marketing jobs, but they didn't happen. I did however learn an awful lot about internet marketing. I also ended up with my "Personal Trainers" certification and a whole bunch of knowledge around nutrition and a passion for healthy living.

In 2013 God unexpectedly opened a number of doors and I went back into selling Real Estate. This was pretty good as it helped me to provide a better income to support the family and it helped me regain some of my battered confidence. Alas, the industry was as rapacious as ever and I struggled swimming against the tide. Real Estate is particularly materialistic and 'successful' people were the lauded ones, even if their personal lives were awful and their ethics dubious. After about four and a half years, I pulled the plug, there had to be a better way to make a living and not get tangled up in petty dramas.

THE SEARCH FOR CHURCH

Our reception after arriving back was nothing short of amazing and I was overwhelmed with people's generosity. In myself there was a constant struggle, I felt totally broken and barely functional. I was puzzled at the warm reception and how much people helped us when we returned, when most had seemed blasé at best when we left. No one had put their hand up to support us, or stayed in contact when we'd needed it in France or Denmark. Hmm..

Looking back and within myself, I was moving away from the 'normal' church model before we left New Zealand to go to France the second time. I was wanting a more spirit lead, "organic", "early church", type of model. A church where everyone participated; everyone came with a psalm, a hymn, a prayer or word of encouragement. There would be no people up front directing things, we all would be responsible for worship and teaching as lead by the Holy Spirit. A transparent, with each other day by day, more intimate type of 'house' church model. Idealistic and optimistic, sure, but from what I'd read and looked at online it was do-able, and the results when it worked, were fantastic.

When we'd arrived in Denmark in 2007, the Vineyard had changed dramatically in the 6 years we'd been away. Arriving back from the crash and burn scene in Paris, we thought the Vineyard would be similar to when we'd left for New Zealand. Not so. The pastor was still a great guy and I respected him immensely, but the focus seemed to be on establishing a large and respected church. The main component of which was to get a building. Unfortunately, past history made him overly protective of "his church" and he seemed to be doing things which gave him more control. It had grown significantly and was more programs focused, less personal, less relational. At the home group that we occasionally went to; the leader openly stated that relationship and intimacy were not what they were there for. (Huh?

RICHARD MULLIGAN

What are you there for then!?). It was still a great place if you liked that style of church, but to me it felt contrived and distant.

As you can imagine this didn't help me adjust or live well in Denmark. It meant I didn't have a mentor or a body of Christian friends to hang out with. It made me question the Western church model, with its numbers, buildings and programs. In my experience, it didn't work well, and certainly wasn't making disciples of all nations.

Back in Cambridge, things had changed in church as well; the leadership had decided their vision was to build a new church building. Alas, this vision was not one I shared and it was with a heavy heart that I told the leader that we'd be leaving. It wasn't a personal or 'doctrine' thing, I respected the leader, liked him, it's just I disagreed with the direction and the focus. I felt I couldn't be part of, or support, something that I felt was heading in a wrong direction.

The focus was on buildings, not the people who actually are 'the church'. I wanted to build up and equip the saints, preach the gospel and make disciples of all nations.

We still wanted fellowship with other believers, so we helped set up a home group with a few other families. We would meet together for dinner on a Saturday, then we'd have a bit of worship and read the Bible together. This went pretty well for about 3 years then one of the main couples went back overseas and after that it slowly spluttered out. Louisa occasionally went to a normal church, usually the Open Brethren in Raleigh St. I was still struggling and didn't want any part of a "bandaid for bullet holes" church or hang out with people who were all 'Facebook' Christians and not vulnerable or real. Harsh judgement, maybe, but I wasn't in the space for playing church, it was the real deal or nothing.

When someone's in a dark hole, struggling with depression and suicidal ideation, some bullshit platitude or a pat on the back just makes it worse. Please, if you think someone is going through a period like that, just come alongside them, let them know you care, let them know you're committed to them. Tell them you don't have the answers, pray with and for them, and listen with all your heart. You may well save their life.

PART 2: WHAT HAVE I LEARNT FROM ALL THIS? THE SEARCH FOR MEANING.

God works in mysterious ways,
his wonders to perform.

Thirteen years after coming back to NZ I still don't understand why things happened the way they did. I've asked many times but no 'understanding' has been forthcoming. I realise God's ways are not my ways and ultimately, he is sovereign in my life and he knows the end from the beginning.

If we are going to trust him to be Lord of our lives, then it's all the way, even when our 'Why Lord?" questions go unanswered. This is hard, really, really hard, trusting God when it doesn't make any sense, particularly when its painful and you've made many sacrifices.

I remember a wise, old missionary giving a talk at Bible College, he said that in the Christian life and following God's will, there will be times where you don't understand what God is doing. What will make it worse is that your 'why God?" questions won't be answered either. That was so true for me in Denmark for those two and a bit years – I had no clue why I was going through it and all my questions remained unanswered. Thirteen years on, my questions remain, but fortunately I have come to a greater acceptance of his sovereignty, and hopefully a better understanding of his character.

I have realised there's no possible way of looking at it from a natural human perspective that is going to make any sense. It hurt, hurts, like crazy - I wouldn't put my worst enemy through the stuff I've been through - and there are some people I really don't like. I realise my brain is way too finite and my understanding too limited, to comprehend why God has allowed me to go through it. There MUST be a divine reason, and it must perfectly fulfil his purposes in me. No matter what my circumstances are, I can trust God's character, that he loves me, he is for me, and he will work it out for good.

Getting to the place of trusting God and letting go of the 'why did those things happen' took many years. It was unbelievably hard, and at times I have despaired. I have been to the end of myself, but I feel like I've come through the most of it now. I still don't understand, but I trust God, and hopefully I will come through these experiences more Christ like. Less of me, and more of him, I rely on him more than ever, it's truly in his strength and not my own. I can ONLY do it through him, if God does not go before me, go with me, then I'm not going at all. I'm too broken and flawed to do anything in my own strength.

Here's a crazy lesson I've discovered; understanding or 'knowing' about your situation, or why it's happening, doesn't actually give you peace. Conversely, having faith and trust in God **does** give you peace. If we can trust in God, committing our lives to him, there is a promise of 'peace which passes all understanding'. Yes please God, can I choose that one.

Life is complex and nuanced

Secondly, I no longer view the world in such black and white terms, there's more grey and even different colours. Dogmatism and pride have taken a beating. I am more compassionate, more understanding of people, particularly foreigners or the marginalised. I know that no matter how awful a train wreck a persons life is - that could be me - but for the grace of God.

I've learnt more about faith

I used to think faith meant to step out boldly and claim whatever it was you were after, it was a pretty straight forward process. I used to expect to be 'rewarded' for those steps of faith, to see the results you were wanting. In the start of my relationship with God, this was somewhat true, God humoured me. Now, it's different, you may not get the result you are expecting or hoping for, because that's not really faith.

Faith is believing and trusting in God and his promises, despite no apparent evidence or results. God will show the way forward - God will guide. Warning! It has never been in the way I have expected Him to guide. It's pretty funny; I have had so many creative ways God could answer my prayers or provide, and guess what, he's never used a single one of them, ever!

The other hard 'faith' lesson is; the 'testing' of your faith. Right in that crucial moment, in the middle of when you don't understand, you don't know why, where circumstances are difficult and painful. Right there, is the test, how strong or big is your faith in God? How do you view the character of God, how's your relationship, not intellectually, but in your heart? Frankly, many times my faith was found wanting, the test was too difficult and I didn't handle it well. Certainly, I never felt like I'd passed, never mind being triumphant.

If God has given us a vision, we can go through many trials, even suffering. As long as we have that God given vision, we can persevere in faith. You can clearly see the 'why' so you can put up with the difficulties on the journey, because you know the destination.

Shortly after I became a Christian I got a glimpse of the vision God had for my life - so It wasn't difficult to give up the whole career thing, to surrender the materialism of a nice new shiny car and house. The comfortable 'successful' life was not difficult to surrender in the anticipation of an adventurous life with Jesus.

As I progressed and pressed into God he gave me a greater purpose that sounded awesome - church planting in France and Paris, (or so I thought). Other ambitions paled into insignificance and as I held onto that vision, it sustained me when faced with ridicule, unbelief, or difficulties. So when that was rudely snatched away, suddenly that underlying sense of purpose and meaning evaporated. I had willingly given up the 'rewards' and trappings of being "successful" to achieve what I thought were the goals God had for me. When the vision was taken away, it left me stunned, in a vacuum, completely at a loss. I was disorientated and confused, it felt like we had been training and building up to run a marathon in Africa and halfway through, when you're going great, suddenly you're playing tennis in Canada, in the winter. You're looking around, wondering what's going on, why's it so dang cold and why am I two sets down already!?

In Denmark, what compounded the difficultly was I felt rejected, judged, and considered of no value. I had very little support and certainly none that understood me, including it seemed, my wife. I suddenly was facing a dramatic change in circumstances, in a different culture, with no preparation, immediately after the Paris dream had crashed and burned. I was a mess of confusion and despair and of course it brought up all the pain and heartache from the past. Those were the darkest days of my life.

LATER, MUCH LATER...

Honestly, after a lot of inner healing, I still don't get it, I flat out still don't understand. Right there, yes right there - in the middle of all that pain and heartache - is the test, how strong or big is your faith in God? What's your heart attitude towards God? Unfortunately, it's a test I've failed many times, but each time I move forward, I trust God a little bit more. I am convinced more than ever, that even if I don't have a clue, I can totally trust God, that he will work things out in my life, for his glory.

In 2017, I read a book which helped. It was "When God breaks your heart" by Ed Underwood. It's an incredible story from a humble guy. It's so real, it addresses the tough issues and asks the questions that you're not supposed to ask God. Like; I can't get angry at God. You can't let it all out with God - somehow that seems blasphemous or sacrilegious. (It's not like God doesn't know what you're thinking anyway!)

He asks the question; why would God let somebody go through very painful and difficult circumstances? In the book you find out he himself is going through some horrific circumstances - I pray I never have to go through the same - I'm not sure I could. I don't know how, but he comes through and he realises that he is strong in his own weakness.

Then in 2020 I read John Bevere's "God Where Are You?" which also helped, though it would have been good to get that message a few years earlier! Then again, I might not have been so open to it earlier. This book gave me some insight into dealing with 'wilderness' times and to stop complaining, like the Israelites had done.

JESUS HAS SET YOU FREE
OF YOUR PAST

I had a dream a few years ago. I was in a medieval type dungeon, filthy, broken, cold, clammy, rank, bound in chains. Suddenly this golden light comes along the corridor and its Jesus. As he comes to the cell door, it opens and my chains drop off, he beckons to come with him, out into the light, I've been set free. Despite the fact that he is so loving, warm and glorious, I hesitate, I know it's awful where I am, but it's all I've known. My eyes have adjusted to the dark, I'm familiar with the pain and deprivation, I know how this goes, I've hardened myself. It's loathsome and full of pain, but it's mine. Can I trust Jesus? what's it even like to be free in the light, it sounds scary, it's unknown.

We are set free of our 'prisons of the past' in Christ, but we need to follow him out into the light. Many of us have trauma in our past, but it does not have to be what defines us. When we are born again into Christ Jesus, we are new creations in Christ according to *2 Corinthians 5:17.*

The past no longer has 'power' over us, it does not have to dominate or influence your present or your future. In Christ, we can leave the past where it is, it doesn't have to rule your life any more. Jesus has set you free, he has removed the chains, he wants to lead you out into the light, to heal you, to give you a hope and a future. Absolutely this is by faith, we need to let Jesus heal us, to bring it all to the cross. Then we can press onward with Jesus, in his power, in his grace.

Let Jesus define who you are. See yourself through God's eyes. If you feel guilt or shame that's not of God! The Holy Spirit brings conviction, which leads to Godly repentance, and restoration of relationship with God. Condemnation, guilt and shame are from the devil, and lead to hiding from God, and moving further away from Him. So I plead with you, leave your past at the foot of the cross, let Jesus give you 'rest for your soul'

THE FUTURE

In the last couple of years I've done a deep dive into the 'end times'. Previously I didn't really care about it - I've always said I'm a Christian because of what God has done in my life here on Earth - he's transformed me here. Heaven was just 'bonus points - bonus lives', I didn't really think about any of that stuff. Recently, as God has lead me into deeper study of the Bible and end times prophecy, I've realised how important it is to understand, albeit it imperfectly, what is coming upon the earth, and our role in it.

When you understand that Jesus' return is imminent, at any moment, its a major motivator to get rid of all the dross and distractions. Clean up and get rid of sin you've left untouched or have let grow. Get right with God, seek his face, and his will for your life. We haven't got time to get bogged down or diverted with anything other than His plan for our lives.

This has radically changed my perspective, earthly ambitions and bucket lists have faded. I want to be engaged and on the spiritual battlefield in these last days. We are on the last straight, the finish line is close, I want to give it everything. There's no point in leaving anything out on the track, no holding back, let's finish the race as strongly as we can.

It has given me an urgency to be about God's business of reaching the lost - to see as many come into the kingdom as possible. I'm praying that God will give me opportunities to talk with people. It's time to take risks, step out in faith, the worst that can happen is you look silly. Believe me, your ego can take the hit. I understand not all of us are comfortable with 'street evangelism' but there are plenty of ways we can engage. The easiest is to pray. The prayers of the righteous are powerful and effective!

We need to set our mind on heavenly things - not earthly things. Our citizenship is in heaven, we are pilgrims and God's ambassadors here on this earth.

My hunger for God has increased dramatically, reading the Bible and prayer have become something I look forward to. The deeper I go, the deeper I want to go, the 'joy of the Lord' has been bubbling up within me at times and it overwhelms me.

PERSPECTIVE

Not long ago, I was beating myself up about my faults and my lack of 'outward' success, I suddenly saw things from a different perspective. What would our lives have been like, what would I have been like, how would things be with my wife and children, if I'd achieved worldly 'success'. I realised that the likely outcome would be missing the mark by a long way, not even close to God's plan for my life . Outwardly all would seemingly be good, perhaps, but my brokenness, the trauma from my childhood, my pride, the fruit of that success, would be corrupted or rotten. I would have been a mess inwardly, and likely relationships broken and scattered. I certainly would not have the inner healing God has given me. Most importantly for me, I suspect my children would be far from God and my focus would be on worldly, not eternal things. I would be a Facebook Christian, a Christian in name only. Inside I would have been miserable and all the coping mechanisms would be going full blast.

I certainly wouldn't have peace, the joy of the Lord, or the comfort that He is with me and for me. That inner peace and joy is priceless, and following Jesus brings the most beautiful fruit, even if i haven't seen it properly yet.

I'll leave you with the Aaronic blessing from Numbers 6:24-26

"The Lord bless you and keep you;

25 The Lord make His face shine upon you,

And be gracious to you;

26 The Lord lift up His countenance upon you,

And give you peace." '

Please feel free to reach out anytime, God Bless you all.

ENJOY THIS BOOK?

You can make a big difference! Independent authors like me rely on you. Reviews are incredibly powerful when it comes to bringing the book to the attention of other readers. Reviews provide 'social proof' that the book isn't a total waste of time.

If you enjoyed this book then I would be grateful if you could take a few minutes and leave me a review on the book's Amazon page. You can jump right to the page by clicking below;

US
UK
Australia
Canada

ABOUT THE AUTHOR

Richard currently lives in New Zealand with his wife and three children. If you'd like to contact Richard you can get him on rich@biblenuggets.nz or you can head to the web site www.biblenuggets.nz for more info.

www.ingramcontent.com/pod-product-compliance
Lightning Source LLC
Chambersburg PA
CBHW071930020426
42331CB00010B/2797